Kyle C.

How to Be An Exceptional Manager

Everything You Need to Know in Mastering the Art of Management

Introduction

This book is part of my career advice series in the IT industries for over 20 years. The content of this book is a compilation of my experience, advice given and shared with my juniors over my years of my career in the aforementioned industry. I started penning down some notes, slides and after some years, the information grew substantially. I thought it might be a waste not to compile them into a book and share it with a wider audience.

The main goal of the book is to share my opinions and insights on what makes a great manager that is able to deliver value to the organisation, command respect from others, loyalty from your own team and of course the job satisfaction for yourself through your great achievements during your career stint. The book will be focusing mainly on the IT industry, but you may find some of the information useful for your industry as well since the role of the manager is pretty similar, that is to ensure that the projects are delivered successfully with minimal hiccups by employing a suitable project management methodology for the project and ensuring the team members are well taken care off to mitigate any risks to the project.

This book is by no means a definite do's and don'ts list for a manager. We, as humans, are gifted with the ability to continuously learn and adapt to new scenarios or environments. But we could still learn a lot from past experiences on what is best for our current settings.Even today I am still exploring new stuff and acquiring new knowledge.

I hope this book could provide useful information in your role as a manager, or getting you ready if you are in the midst of getting promoted to the management role.

With that being said, I hope you enjoy this book.

Before we dive in deep into the topic, we ought to ask ourselves this basic question, the very question that brought you to this book.

What is the job of a Manager?

By common definition, the role and function of a manager within an organisation or a company is to lead and oversee a team or department. Managers within an organisation are responsible for planning, organising, coordinating, and directing the team's efforts to achieve goals and objectives laid out by the top management. The key functions of a manager include communicating expectations, providing guidance, as well as making correct decisions to ensure efficient operations and effective performance of the team. Managers would assist HR in recruiting and developing team members according to the needs, resolve problems with other stakeholders, and adjusting to changes in the business environment. There are times where the manager would need to resolve conflicts between the team members or departments.

Managers play a vital role in creating a positive work culture, promoting collaboration, and representing the team's interests to higher management and stakeholders. Overall, the manager's role is crucial in achieving success, maximising productivity, and fostering a supportive and inclusive work environment for those under the manager's supervision.

Misconception about being a Manager

There are many misconceptions about being a manager. Tonnes of newcomers to the job are vying for the manager positions a few years after into their career because they thought being a manager would be a cushy job that comes with a lot of perks. Once getting the role of the manager, they would just need to sit there and direct other teams to do the job while they will be acting as the supervisor to monitor the tasks being carried out. In reality, being a manager is the complete opposite. It is a stressful job that challenges both physically and mentally.

Here are some of the common misconceptions about being a manager:

- **Managers have more power and authority**

  While managers do have some degree of authority bestowed by the company to carry out their responsibility effectively, they must work within the constraints of company policies, budgets, and according to the decisions made by the upper management. The managers are not allowed to cross the red line of their role. As the saying goes, "*With great power comes great responsibility*" the manager would often have to take on many hats in a team, as opposed to a regular team member who can just focus on his own assigned tasks.

- **Managers just give orders and delegate**

    It is true that managers give orders and delegate
    tasks to their team members since their role is to
    oversee the entire project or team to ensure good
    productivity and results from the team. However,
    effective management involves much more than
    giving orders. Good managers lead by example,
    have proper planning, support their team, and
    collaborate with team members to achieve common
    goals. A manager is often required to have the
    expertise and knowledge on the field since having
    those skills would allow the manager to quickly
    identify problems within a project and immediately
    prepare possible solutions to the many scenarios that
    might occur within a project.

- **Managers have the final say**

    A lot of managers expect the team members to
    follow their orders to the letter . Their commands are
    absolute and no team member should challenge
    them. Humans make mistakes all the time. We are
    not all-knowing and perfect. Therefore, managers do
    often make mistakes, and sometimes these mistakes
    could lead to a more serious problem since the
    managers' decision could affect the entire project.
    As managers, they must be willing to seek input
    from the team, consult with experts, and collaborate
    to make informed decisions to better manage the
    project risks. In fact, the real decision makers are

often the business units, stakeholders or project sponsors. The managers are there to carry out their will and execute all the decisions that were made in the top level meetings.

- **Promotion to manager means a pay raise with many perks along the way**

  While it's true that managerial positions often come with added responsibilities and some perks that come with the position, not all promotions lead to an immediate pay increase. In some cases, the added workload may come with a different compensation structure. Managers might be given special allowance such as phone allowance, or meal/ entertainment allowance for them to conduct their job better, especially if they need to interact with clients. In some cases, those managers get very little increments in their base salary after being given the fixed allowances by the company.

- **Managers have more free time**

  Managers have the exact opposite of that. Effective managers often have demanding schedules as they would need to facilitate meetings with various parties to ensure that correct information and expectations are being passed to the parties involved in the projects. They need to prepare the presentations as well as progress updates to the top management and are responsible for both their own work and overseeing the work of their team members, which can be time-consuming and mentally taxing. Therefore, managers who claim that they have more free time are not doing their job properly.

- **Managers are always in control**

    On the contrary, managers are always **NOT** in control due to the unpredictable situations and uncertainties when managing the project or the team. For example, the stakeholders might suddenly change the requirements at the last minute or the top performer in the team called in a long sick leave. Therefore, they must be able to adjust to changing circumstances and may not always have complete control over all aspects of their team's performance as well as having a good risk management practice in place.

- **Being promoted as a manager means I have good leadership qualities**

    Leadership doesn't come by just being a manager. It is a skill that requires development and continuous improvement by the individual. Not all managers are automatically effective leaders, and leadership qualities need to be cultivated. Many were promoted due to their connections with their superiors, creating many incompetent managers who would lead to many failed projects, true story.

- **Managers focus solely on the bottom line**

While achieving business objectives is essential, good managers also prioritise the well-being and growth of their team members. Manager would need to handle conflicts, career advancement needs and cultivate a good working environment for the team apart from managing the day to day operations and projects.

- **Managers are disconnected from day-to-day tasks**

Effective managers stay involved and are aware of the team's work. They understand the challenges faced by their team and offer support when needed. Usually good managers would conduct periodic sessions with the team members to find out if the team if facing any obstacles or impediments for the project, as well as the mental well-being of the team to ensure that everyone has the opportunity to voice out their opinions, difficulties and issues which might require intervention of the manager to resolve them.

- **Managers can't be friends with their subordinates**

While maintaining a professional boundary is important, it is vital for managers to develop strong, positive relationships with their team members to promote good teamwork and foster a supportive work environment. When in need, the entire team will stand in to provide their 100% support behind the manager rather than having a fragmenting team constantly bickering with the manager until it poses significant morale problems to the entire team or department.

The goal of the manager is to ensure successful delivery of the project within a reasonable timeframe, costs and meeting expectations of the stakeholders. A manager cannot just focus on delivering a project on time, but sacrifice quality which sadly is often the case. The project delivered must meet a reasonable threshold that is agreeable and accepted by all stakeholders. Imagine if you hired a contractor to renovate your house. The contractor assured that he is able to deliver your requirements within the stipulated time frame, or even earlier within the budget. While he is able to uphold his promise, the work quality is bad enough that things would start falling apart after a while. On the other hand, if the contractor is doing a great job at delivering high quality work but is taking forever to complete the project because the contractor is a perfectionist who would repaint the entire wall just because he found the paint in some spots were uneven. Lastly, there is a contractor who is able to deliver the project within the timeframe and excepted quality, but overruns the budget because he needed to hire extra and purchase resources to get the project done on time. Which of the scenarios above is acceptable to you as the customer? The answer is None. Because you would not want to get something that is of bad quality, or taking too long to complete or have to fork out extra from your original budget. You just need to plan out all the things you aim to achieve into milestones or prepare a roadmap to keep track of what you want to achieve so you can pace it according to your budget and time.

Being a manager are the dreams of many workers who just started their career. There is a high percentage of junior staff who I have worked with said they hope to be promoted to a managerial position within two to three years time. When I asked them why they were aiming for this as there are other ways to advance your career, for example being a specialist or becoming a consultant, or moving up to be an advanced engineer. Their answers were simple, they want to be able to control others and delegate the tasks while enjoying all the perks that come with the positions.

This is a major misconception that managers are there to just tell others what to do and sit in their office or cubicles doing no work. If you have come across this type of manager, then you are being unlucky to have a supervisor who is abusing his or her position. This culture has created a bad perception to those good, hardworking workings while creating a twisted goal for the bad eggs who are horrible at their work to try to move up to the manager positions to escape all the complaints from their co-workers for being bad at their jobs or getting berated by their supervisor.

In truth, being a manager is not as easy as many would like to think. I have seen many new managers yelling out the famous line from Palpatine from the Revenge of the Sith, *"Power!!! Unlimited Powerrrrr!!!"* when they first started the new role. They felt like they have all the power in the world to move the team members like chess pieces. They prefer to dabble in office politics more than actually managing the team or the projects, just because it is more interesting than the boring, mundane job of preparing the progress update to the top management and solving actual problems. These "managers" would often forget that their role carries huge responsibilities in ensuring the optimal performance of the team and delivering those projects within the budget and timeline. In reality, how often do we see projects getting delayed and the managers or department heads are blaming each other for the problems?

Common Traits of A Bad Manager

1. A bad manager is a horrible micromanager

A bad manager will manage his or her staff to the smallest details. The staff members usually will not have any say or any channel to voice out their opinions, even if they know that the decisions or requests from the manager will lead to undesirable consequences. The staff members will be under constant, excessive supervision by their manager. A bad micromanager will often provide criticisms to the work by the staff members. Nothing seems to satisfy the manager no matter what the staff did, if it is not as per the exact steps or requirements by the micromanager.

I have seen and worked with many micromanagers throughout my career. These managers would interfere in every single detail of the work done by their staff. For example, I had a manager, which I considered as the worst micromanager that I have seen in my life, would criticise the font style and size used in my presentation. She would then ask me to change it and send it back to her. When I finally did it, she would change her mind and asked me to change it back to the original one as it looked more presentable, after she had seen the new changes. When I sent her the progress update for my team, she would criticise that it lacked certain information and would request me to follow her template. After I had done exactly that, she did not even present the "additional" information that she had requested from me to her boss as it was not even deemed relevant or important by her boss. She just wanted to have it because she wants it to be in her template.

Another staff member of mine got a far worse experience than me. He wasn't feeling well that day and had to make frequent visits to the loo. He had bad diarrhoea that day. When that lady manager found out that he kept "disappearing" from his desk, she "interrogated" him mercilessly. After finding out his condition, she did not even ask the staff to take a medical leave to rest. Instead, she started to time the staff, giving him only 10 minutes per trip to the restroom, and focused on monitoring his work for the rest of the day. Worse off, she even gave more work to that poor staff to complete, and making tonnes of change requests along the way.

The main reason why managers like to micromanage, from my observation, is to have the satisfaction of having power over someone else. The micromanager would think doing so will command the respect and exert his or her authority over his team. When there is only one voice to be heard, the team can move together in sync, according to the will of the manager, and it will get things done according to plan, or that is what they think. While this strategy might have worked early on, but as time passes, it will just lead to severe demoralisation of the staff members, and even generating hatred among the team members towards the micromanager after all the oppression and being treated like a machine or a prisoner over the years. The staff members would not hesitate to leave the team for another department, or for another company after securing a new position. There was a manager who was a bad micromanager and ended up losing the entire department because of his autocratic style. His reputation was so bad that no one would want to join his department which ended up being merged with another department, and he lost his job since his department was made redundant.

2. A bad manager doesn't listen to others.

A bad manager who doesn't listen to others usually comes with a big ego. It is an inseparable package for managers with this kind of trait. Perhaps it is to hide their incompetence, which often backfired as others would easily see through that cover because this type of manager always makes the same, stupid mistake. The motto, "my way or the highway", is their only principle guiding them in their career. They would allow no voices other than theirs to be heard. They would allow no orders other than theirs to be executed. Any difference in opinions and suggestions will be stemmed out, with those who dared to voice out different opinions penalised. They will make you bend to their will and become their "yes man " one way or the other. The saddest thing is that there are many managers out there with this trait that are screwing hundreds, if not millions of good staff who just wanted to offer some honest opinions out there, including myself when I was a junior staff. I had the opportunity to work with many of these scums, with the ones that combined with the micromanager trait being the worst of the lots.

So back to my previous manager mentioned above, apart from being a horrible micromanager, she tried to portray herself as the "know-it-all", when in reality she wasn't any expert at all in any aspects. She had no experience in managing a team specialising in system design. Yet, she was the head of the digitisation department that requires tremendous knowledge in the business and technology to create solutions that would help to bring value to the company. She never once asks the opinions of others before making a decision that would impact the entire team or the company. For example, she would pluck a deadline from the sky before consulting the team who would be doing the actual work. More often than not, she would set a ridiculous timeline and force the team to work additional hours to commit to that timeline that wasn't agreed by the team. If she somehow managed to force the team and somehow got the project delivered according to that timeline, then she would get all the glory in front of the bosses. To top it off, she would always decide on a feature before getting the feedback from the compliance team. A good system or a solution would need to adhere to certain regulations and compliance so it would not pose any risks when the system is rolled out for public use, particularly in the areas of security and data protection. As usual, she managed to disregard all the advice and feedback from her own team, who knew that the feature that she insisted to be included in the system would have severe repercussions later. The feature she wanted would compromise the customers' data security. Many others, including the developers have raised the security risks countless times as well. Somehow she managed to bulldoze it through by invoking the names of the upper management to make those against her ideas submit to her forcefully. When shit hit the fan after customers started lodging complaints over the feature, she would use the "Blame others" card in her arsenal, complaining that the IT and the Compliance team did not voice out regarding the problem.

3. Stealing the work of others and taking credit for his or herself.

A bad manager is often the selfish, narcissist git who cares nothing about others but himself. Any team achievements are solely because of his or her brilliance guiding, or should I put it, "misguiding-but-others-totally-ignored-the-nonsense" the team. Most of the bad managers I have come across many managers would blatantly steal the credits and hard work of their own team members.

This type of managers often lacked the required skills and knowledge for the position, but had to steal credit in order to secure their positions that they had stolen from deserving candidates through lies and deceit. They often feel insecure and paranoid that they will be replaced by another person who is able to perform well and display that success in front of the management. Hence, they would suppress the team to prevent them from having any chances to have their own moments. The easiest method would be stealing ideas for credit later since they are not capable of doing the tasks themselves.

Their despicable act did not just end at stealing ideas from their own team. When they did not receive positive feedback from the ideas that they have stolen from their staff, especially in front of the big bosses, they would brush it off and blame it on their team for not doing enough research before presenting it to the management. It is never their own fault. For them, the team is there to make them look good, not otherwise, despite the fact that they were the one stealing the idea without first trying to understand the idea. Some even went further by modifying the proposal.I would find those who lacked decent intelligence and common sense to be most amusing. They would just steal the ideas without knowing if it would fit for the problem.

There was this manager who was great with office politics where he alone was responsible for 80% of the drama in the office, but severely lacked the technical knowledge for his position as the Digital Solutions Manager. He got the promotion because he is a sweet talker that managed to "captivate" the hearts of one of the directors. He knew that he could only grab onto his position by continuously feeding on the work from others. Otherwise his cover to disguise his own incompetence would be blown and he could be replaced by another staff member very soon. As such, he would often steal the ideas from his team to present in our monthly innovation meeting, to show that he fits for the role.

The monthly innovation meeting was an important meeting where all the key figures in the company, including the c-levels would be present. All department heads would be sending in someone to pitch an idea for a new product, business transformation and what not, as long as the idea would greatly benefit the company. It was a golden opportunity for any level to shine in front of the top management, if they manage to present great ideas that could gain their attention. Other departments would send in their top guns to present new ideas and proposals. Some were collective ideas presented by the team leader, others were presented by the entire team to show great teamwork. This manager however, would ask his team to prepare the presentation slide for him, and then modify the content to claim as his own. Because he lacked the knowledge, and was too lazy to perform some basic research on Google, he would distort the content of the slide into something that is ridiculous and laughable.

In one of the innovation meetings, he completely embarrassed himself during the presentation. As the company was going through the digital transformation process in digitising all the paperwork at the branches, the company was discussing having a solution by creating a mobile app for customers to scan and submit the data over at the terminals that will be set up at the branches. At any given time, customers could come in, use the mobile app to interact with the terminals using the internet from their own cellular network without the need to queue up at the counters. The "smart"manager replaced all the words,"cellular network" with "WiFi", so he could claim credit for the proposal from his team. So the presentation turned out to be "Customers will be connecting to the terminal through the Wifi". When the CTO asked how would the mobile users subscribe to this "WiFi" and who would be the service provider, he was taken by surprise. He started giving nonsense by proposing setting up public Wifi for the customers to use, which would be an additional cost to the company, especially where there are hundreds of branches and the branches already have existing staff to assist customers who might have difficulty in using the mobile app.

To save face, he started defending the indefensible, spurting out more garbage, claiming that each customer will have his or her own "wifi" when visiting the branch, because the "Telcos" would provide them with the "public Wifi". He even started "demonstrating" it on his phone. In the end, the CTO had enough of his stupidity and asked him, "*Do you know what a cellular network vs wifi connection is?*" Other managers who he had beef with began to laugh maniacally, obviously taking the chance to brutally attack his credibility. Even the director was hiding his face behind his hand while shaking his head at his "Protégé".

The presentation ended disastrously as one would expect, amplified by the merciless attacks from the audience. Soon, the news spread and he became a laughing stock in the company. Some even gave him the nickname, "Wifi-John" for the debacle. Still, he was shameless enough to be present in the upcoming meetings, and continued to steal and present "interesting" ideas that he had modified much to our amusement.

As a general rule, credit must be given when it is due. It is just basic respect and appreciation to those who came up with the effort or ideas. You will be seen as a big hearted person and a good manager with top notch leadership skills who are able to groom your team members. The manager would get the attention and the credit for being able to lead a top performing team. With this, he or she would never need to steal the credits from others in order to survive in office politics.

4. A bad manager would always blame others

"*I can do no wrong because I am a manager.*" This was the quote from my previous manager when I was a junior programmer when the decision made by the manager did not go according to plan.

A bad manager always blames others when things are not going according to his or her desire, or if terrible consequences occur, thanks to his or her "brilliant" decisions. You might think that you could defend yourself by presenting the facts and evidence to counter the blame, you are wrong. This type of manager is like "a slippery snake that is further oiled and lubricated", who could slip through any attempt to trap them into admitting his or her own mistakes, even as insurmountable evidence were presented in front of him or her. A manager of this trait usually could create tons of excuses and have the ability to find faults in others to shift the blame to them when there is a chance.

Let's take the same example from the previous manager who wanted to have the feature that would compromise the data security of customers since there is a continuation to the story. When the customers' complaint started flooding in, she deflected the responsibility to the system designer and programmers for allowing this feature to be added in the final product. Initially she thought she could use her position as a manager to silence the critics, but her action only further added fuel to the fire.The enraged system designer and programmers took matters into their own hands and countered her effort to push the blame to them. They produced the email trail of their discussions, along with the recordings taken from the meetings where she was "using the names of the higher ups" to pressure the team into adding this feature to the higher management. Still, she was unperturbed. She shifted the blame to the security risk and compliance team, blaming that team for failing to filter out the features that could pose security risks before the system is deployed to production, when in fact, as the manager for the project, it was her job to ensure that she got the consensus and approval from all the departments before even starting the development. She could not produce any official sign offs from the respective departments except her own for the release.

Fortunately for her, but an unfortunate event for the company, she was let off the hook as she had someone in the top management covering up for her. In the end, the security risk and compliance team took the blame and responsibility for the problem with the excuse that they are the last gatekeeper before anything can be released to production. The engineering teams had to pay the price for it, by working extra hours to rectify the problem. Her behaviour had caused severe resentment towards her from those who took the blame. For the upcoming projects, no one was there to provide the support for her. No one would respond to her meeting requests. Even when she escalated to the upper management, they would just "show face" without providing any real value during discussions in the meeting. They had all ganged up to revolt against her, with the intention to make feel isolated and eventually get her to resign. But alas, she was one of the "court favourites" of the director and from what I heard from the staff who still works at that company, she is still surviving and continues to wreak havoc there. Those who I have worked with have long departed from that "living hell", with many more staff joining but leaving the company after a short stint because of her.

5. Politician and a good "Brown-Noser"

A good manager understands the importance of establishing good connections with others to ensure smooth sailing of the projects under him. A bad manager however, will establish his or her network of influence for his or her agenda. A good manager is a diplomat, while a bad manager is a selfish, despicable politician. Bad managers know how to please their bosses and curry their favours. In return, their bosses might turn a blind eye to some of the problems created by them, or provide support to them even when they have suggested a stupid suggestion.

From my long career experience, I have seen way too many "arse-licker" and was personally screwed by such a manager a couple times. It began with a meeting and my head of department at that time was the favourite of the General Manager. My team at that time was responsible for proposing new product features to the current systems. The role was different from business analysts as our job was to gather feedback, perform competitor analysis, research on the market trends and then brainstorm to suggest new features to the existing systems or we will request the IT department to build a new system to support our new initiatives. We were the "Digital Transformation Consultants" in the company. Usually after our analysis, we would prepare the detailed requirements for the business analysts from the IT department to review our proposals on how or which system would incorporate those functions in, since the business analysts are the bridge between us, who are part of the business stakeholders, with the development team. That was the role given, or stated in our job description when we signed the dotted line on the employment offer. The team consists of professionals from various backgrounds, including those with strong technical knowledge, like solution architects, programmers, etc, as we need to have such skills to deeply understand the systems from other competitors, or even identify the problems in the existing design in order to propose the solution that will be implemented. You could consider the team as a mini IT department on its own but we would merely be acting as consultants. The job of implementing our proposal would still rest under the IT department, that was what we were told. The team was a new team formed by the company to break out from the traditional IT department where issues can be looked at from different perspectives by various professionals to increase the competitiveness of the company's products.

The new manager who was leading the new team had limited knowledge on almost anything. Furthermore, she never joined any discussions or brainstorming sessions, unless the big bosses were in those meetings. She never initiated any weekly team meetings to provide us with the management direction, requirements, visions and what not. We would only discover it through another party that wasn't part of our department. Perhaps she thought it would be a waste of time mingling with the lower level staff. She preferred to be seen and "polishing" the shoes of the higher ups. One day, she went full force on her "brown-nosing" skills. Eager to earn more favours from the top management, she took on jobs that were supposed to be under the IT department. A project was slightly delayed due to insufficient resources from the IT department at that time, no thanks to department heads that cared nothing more than ridiculous timelines set by plucking figures from the sky without any consultation with the people who are actually doing the job. At that time, all the projects were running in parallel, with new projects coming in with the same deadline given for other projects. The PMO team did not even have an overview of all the projects that were running concurrently. Even if they had it, they wouldn't even dare to present it because the head of the PMO, along with most of the PMs, were "yes-man". The office politics were awful with department heads fighting one another for favours, rather than doing actual work that would improve the company.

This situation gave an opening for my manager to please the higher ups. During one of the meetings, she proposed to have me leading some of the projects on behalf of the IT team, since they were short of hands, and I have the required skills to manage a project. Initially, it would be fine as I wouldn't mind helping out other departments in need, but it should be a one time business. The projects went live successfully within reasonable time and my manager took all the credits for her brilliant suggestion that led to this. After getting the praises from the bosses like a good, obedient poodle, she then put the team on the customer support role for post production support. The team had to actually work as the customer service support when there was already a customer service department performing the same function. The project management and customer support work became permanent after this. The team was dismantled after 6 months because everyone in the team had left as everyone was doing the tasks that were not part of the job scope stated in their contracts.

6. A bad manager spreads fire instead of saving or putting out the fire

Bad managers are usually incompetent, that is a fact. Most of the time, they move their way up the organisation ladder by being the brown-nosers and becoming the loyal pet for the higher ups, while sacrificing many of their colleagues along the way. They developed the wrong skills over the years. Instead of focusing on their social skills to work with their teams through good communication and transparency, they prefer to use intimidations and lies to solidify their position within the company. They lead the path of destruction, rather than the path of peace and harmony. The phrase "good teamwork" is akin to the holy blessings onto the foul demons. They despise the great office culture where everyone works well with one another. They feared the project could be delivered without any dramas as they would lose their source of importance. Have you ever encountered a situation where the project went smoothly with very minor or no hiccups and the manager who has never shown up in any discussions or meetings suddenly turned up and changed the requirements at the last minute?

This same manager also appeared out of nowhere during my online training to all the regional staff on the new system that we will be launching within a week. Mind you, the audience count was around 200 plus people on Teams, many of them were division heads and senior managers. My manager who joined halfway through the call, when I had finished answering the questions from the audience during the first few topics, began scolding the audience after noticing that they did not ask any questions to me. Mind you, I had just done it minutes before he joined. He then left the online conference call, with the excuse that he is a busy person and had other important meetings to attend. Before leaving, he said that he would lodge a complaint with the General Manager stating that they were not being interactive in the training session. The audience were stunned by the sudden scolding from nowhere and were left completely speechless. This idiot has effectively made enemies with all the regional managers and staff. After the session, I had to clean up the mess or our team can never get any support or assistance from them in the future for future project rollouts. This wasn't the only time where the manager started a shit storm. During the next project meeting with another department, that manager wanted the other department to agree to his proposal, despite facing objections from most of the staff as his proposal did not resolve the operation issues raised by the operation and the customer service departments. Frankly put, it was a dumb idea. The IT department has counter-proposed a different proposal that would resolve most of the existing problems and customer complaints. As you might have guessed, there is no way in hell that the manager would agree to it because it wasn't his proposal. If the project is successful, he would not get any credit for it. Therefore, he needed to force the majority to submit to his will. He needed the project to use all his ideas so he could claim all the credits. That manager soon began the spree of spreading defamation and lies about the IT team. He even managed to convince the operation and customer service teams to adopt his solution, telling them that the proposal from the IT department was just a means to get rid of them through system automation. The moment anyone touches on the livelihood of someone, all hell breaks loose.

Both the operation and customer service teams began to boycott the solution from the IT department that was meant to reduce the workload and human errors. The issue escalated throughout the company and sparked a war between IT and the Operation team where both sides would start yelling at each other in the meetings. The situation got so bad until the COO had to intervene and call off that project entirely in order to calm all the parties.The only good thing that came out of this was that the COO did not adopt the solution from that manager, which helped to avert another war should the company go ahead with that implementation.

7. Does not have any empathy

A bad manager doesn't care about his or her own staff. The most important thing is about his or her own agenda. Nothing else matters to them. When the staff is having difficulties in completing his task, the bad manager would never even care to find out the issue or the root cause that is plaguing the staff. Instead, the bad manager will continue to pressure the staff to complete his or her work by threatening the staff, fearing that any delays would delay the project, which in turn would jeopardise or affect his or her reputation in front of the bosses. This type of manager would have no hesitation in sacrificing the team in order to create the illusion that all is well with the project.

I have seen a staff member who had developed anxiety problems and subsequently suffered from a mental breakdown during a project because of the actions from the bad manager. The staff was a new joiner who has yet familiarised himself with the business and operations. On his first day at work, his manager just threw a whole new project that is not small, with a ridiculous timeline for him to complete. Worse off, the manager did it without providing any sort of project briefing on how to start the project, what are the requirements or any documentation. Heck, the manager did not even introduce the project stakeholders to the new guy. The new staff was left with much confusion. He had no idea where to start. When he approached the manager for information, he was only given this amazing advice, "*You need to figure it out yourself. You are a grown up man for fuck's sake*," I apologised for the obscenity in the sentence, but this was the actual words uttered by that manager. That manager even told the new staff if he fails to complete the project on time it would mean failing his probation and he would not be accepted as a permanent staff member. Imagine you had these words uttered to you on your first day at work. Later I found out that the project was going to fail anyways because of the gross miscommunications between the departments and horrible requirements that had already caused significant delays to the project timeline. The person in charge of the project? You guessed it right? That manager, and now he is looking for a scapegoat to push the blame and responsibilities to the newcomer.

In the end the new staff resigned just after two weeks into the job as he did not receive any support and assistance from his manager. Who wouldn't? I think anyone would have done so if he or she was left treated like a stranger within the team.I have had the chance to chat with the new guy and found that he was quite knowledgeable in his field. But I did not tell him about the horrible politics and the scheme by his manager so he would not leave the place with a deep scar. If only he was given the proper guidance and support, he could perhaps be the top performer for the team. But alas, because of the inept manager who cares little for his subordinate, the company lost what could be a good staff. A crude diamond waiting to be polished. Yet, the manager was lamenting how it was difficult for him to hire new staff for his team. Perhaps he should look into the mirror to find out the root cause. This was something I wish I could tell him in the face, but then it could spark a diplomacy row between the departments as he was a court favourite of one of the directors in the company.

A manager with no empathy would eventually bring the sense of rejection, the feeling of disgust from his or her own teammates. No team members would respect the manager's authority. The team performance would see a steady decline as no one would be giving their 100% for their work as they know the harder they work, they would be penalised with more work with a higher target since the manager does not care about their wellbeing. They would be squeezed for results in order for the manager to please the higher ups. If you lack empathy towards your staff, perhaps it is a good time to reflect on it before the revolution starts among your team members.

8. Biased and do not promote team members according to merit

A good manager would always promote staff who have displayed good performance, merit and contributed to the team. A bad manager would prefer to promote those who have shown loyalty and obey every of his or her command. The goal of the good manager is teamwork to produce great results for the company, so that the manager could negotiate better incentives, salary increments and bonuses for the staff during the annual performance review. The bad manager, on the other hand, is all about power and position to further his or her own agenda. The bad manager would need to build his or her own support base for power. Those who performed well might be seen as a threat to the bad manager, unless of course, that top performer is willing to become a brown-noser to the manager. Incentives, bonuses, and promotions became a tool for the bad manager to secure and demand obedience from his or her staff members. Producing results is the last and the least important objective for the team. I have seen some bad managers threaten the team to obey his command without questioning, even if it is a stupid order that would bring bad consequences to the team. If they objected, he would exercise the "power given to him" at his discretion, even if the team performed remarkably well.

Never see your team members under your supervision as mere pawns to advance your agenda. If you treat them well with respect, and cultivate the culture of rewarding them according to merits, the team would function well and produce good results for the team. There won't be a need for any office politics as the company would give more attention to the teams which could drive better results and revenue for the company. Afterall, making money is the most important aspect in any business. Throughout my career as the manager of a team or a department, I would let the team results to speak for itself. Even if others are trying to discredit me or my team, my CEO at the time would not entertain such gossip or disinformation. I was granted full autonomy to run my department, as long as my department is producing results and bringing in healthy revenue for the company. If you are doing all these and the boss of the company sided with the bad side of the group, perhaps it is time to look elsewhere and move on.

8. Acting like a messenger, and a bad one as well

There are a lot of managers that I have worked with that were awful messengers, to the point of providing a message that is completely different from the original message.
The role of a manager is not only ensuring that the team is able to function well and achieve the goals and objectives set by the upper management, he or she has to make sure that the directives or information given is accurate so that the team can work towards the objectives. Many a times, especially in a project environment, a bad manager with this awful trait would just be passing information around without first filtering the messages.When a project manager behaves in this manner, it could bring a lot of issues to the team and also increase the project risks.The manager who are bad messengers are often than not, lack the skills of critical thinking. The total absence of these key skills would often cause great confusion among the team members, and the irritation of key stakeholders or clients.

I have worked with one project manager who had neither the critical thinking skills nor common sense and was one of the worst messengers ever. All of the projects involving this guy would either be delayed or failed after launch. Why?

- The project manager did not know how to plan for the project. He would often rely on others to tell him what to do. Sometimes he even passes the task to a junior staff member from the business unit to plan it for him.

- The project manager lacked the skills and knowledge to manage the project as he did not even understand the requirements, either business or technical aspects of it. He could only assist in arranging the meetings. Even with that simple task, he would often screw it up as meeting invites to the stakeholders were sent during the last minute, or his meeting arrangements would clash or overlap with other meetings, creating huge confusions to others.

- The project manager would often skip the meetings or leave between the meetings, resulting in the loss of information in his meeting minutes. In some cases, vital information and follow ups were omitted since he was not in the meeting to take note of those items during the discussions. This often causes delays to the projects because information was not up to date and developers would have to either wait for the project manager to conduct the follow up sessions in order to deliver the correct expectations to the stakeholders or risk revamping the solution because of the new requirements from those sessions.

- The project manager would often distort the information based on his own interpretation in order to fill in the gaps from his frequent "disappearances" at important discussions. Because he lacked the skills and knowledge, the end result was always disastrous. Meeting minutes and project documentations were full of problems and conflicting information. There were many instances where the technical teams delivered the wrong implementation because of the information given. As a result, many of his projects steered from the actual requirements from the business owners and the developers would have to make last minute changes or sometimes revamping the solution because of the wrong requirements given to them by the project manager.

Strong communication and delivering the precise and accurate message is key to any project. A project typically involves business stakeholders that wanted something and the delivery team would execute the business requirement to produce the end result. While a business analyst is the glue between the business teams and the delivery teams to ensure that the requirements are translated correctly to the final product, the product manager is the supervisor that oversees the entire machinery. Communication is like the flow of electricity to various parts of the machines so that each part can perform properly. If the wrong current or the current is not provided to the components, what do you think will happen to the production?

So what are the qualities that a good manager should have?

A good manager typical has the following skills and traits:

1.   Clear Communication:

As given in the example previously, good communication is key in managing a team or a project. A good manager always communicates clearly and effectively with their team. They convey instructions, expectations, and feedback in an understandable manner. Regular team meetings are conducted and the manager provides transparent updates to the team members so they are well informed at all times.

For example, the manager holds a team meeting to discuss project goals and assigns tasks with clear instructions. During the meeting, they encourage team members to ask questions and provide feedback to avoid any misunderstandings. When they are being informed of a change in company directions or objectives, they will immediately update the team members so everyone is aligned and on the same page to avoid misalignment issues that might lead to resource wastage and even conflicts.

2. Empathy

Effective managers show great empathy and understanding towards their team members. They are sensitive to their needs, concerns, and personal situations, fostering a supportive work environment. They are always ready to listen to the problems before coming to a conclusion or decisions. If the team members know that their manager is empathetic to their concerns or problems, and giving them the flexibility to resolve their problems, they would be more productive at work since they can focus on their work without having to worry too much as they could raise it to their manager and obtain his or her understanding.

For example: When a team member faces personal challenges, the manager listens empathetically and offers support whenever they can to the team member. They may grant some flexibility in work hours or provide resources to help the team member manage their workload during the difficult time as long as it is within their authority and jurisdiction. If not, they would seek advice and escalate to the level above to help out the team member so that the issue can be resolved and that the team member can focus on work.

3. Supportive

A good manager supports their team by providing necessary resources, guidance, and encouragement to help them succeed in their roles and reach their potential. The manager is not stingy with the knowledge and skills that they have accumulated over the years, and would groom the juniors within the team so that they may advance further and be better in their career. The manager would step in to defend the team members if they are in the right, but not to the level of increasing the conflicts or problems.

For example, the manager identifies team members' career aspirations and arranges for relevant training and professional development opportunities. The manager would offer guidance and mentorship to assist team members in their growth. The team's well being, performance and productivity are the main concern of the manager and he or she will always be there for the team when they need their manager.

4.   Strong Leadership

Good managers with strong leadership skills will always lead by example and inspire their team to achieve their best. They set a positive tone for the workplace and motivate others to excel. They will make sure the team is always moving towards the same, common goal and make decisive actions without hesitations. They are the go to person for advice, guidance. They are the key pillar that puts together the entire team.

As an example, a manager who exhibits the quality of strong leadership, when the time comes for a challenging project, the manager remains optimistic and leads the team with confidence. He or she provides encouragement, acknowledges team members' efforts, and celebrates small wins to boost morale. The manager would lead the team through any obstacles and steer the team towards success.

5.   Decisiveness

Managers need to make decisions regularly, and being able to do so decisively and confidently is crucial for the team's progress. If a manager is incapable of taking decisive actions, not only does it delay the progress of the project, the manager would be seen as a weak leader who is not capable of leading. Team members will start losing the trust and judgement of such managers and might begin to make their own decisions without consulting the manager. As a result, the manager would start to lose control of the team and the project alike, making the manager redundant and the first in line for termination if the company decides to reduce the headcount since the manager carries no value. The project and the team would continue to run with or without the presence of that manager.

As an example: When faced with two equally viable options for a project direction, the manager weighs the pros and cons, considers team input, and makes a well-informed decision to move the project forward. If mistakes were made, the manager would be able to resolve the issues and take immediate and necessary steps to steer the project back to the correct direction.

6.   Problem-Solving Skills

Effective managers are adept at identifying and solving problems that arise within the team or the organisation. They fully understand if the problems are not tackled and resolved immediately, it may snowball into a more serious problem, posing significant risks to the project. Managers with this trait are often sharp, having great common sense and good logical thinking skills. They would first analyse the root cause of the problems and the many ways on how to resolve them, with the various scenarios and end result being simulated in their brains. On the other hand, managers who lacked this skill would often ignore the problems raised until they got so bad and complicated that required the involvement from the top management. This would mean that some innocent but capable bystander had to clean up the entire mess.

Example: When the team encounters a roadblock in a project, the manager facilitates a brainstorming session, encouraging creative thinking to find viable solutions. The manager would provide all the problems, root cause analysis and possible solutions to these problems.
After getting the feedback required, the manager would then work with the team to implement the chosen solution.

7. Delegation

Good managers always know how to delegate tasks to the right individuals based on their skills and strengths. They trust their team members to carry out their responsibilities on their own. Contrary to a micromanager, the manager will never try to take over the job of the member or force the team members to deliver according to the instructions. Instead, the manager would empower the team members to work on their tasks delegated based on what they think is best. If mistakes are committed, or the team members had ventured off from the objective of their tasks, the manager would immediately point it out to the team and provide the necessary guidance for them to get back on track.

Example: The manager delegates tasks according to each team member's expertise. For instance, they assign a team member with strong presentation skills to represent the team in an important client meeting. Then having the team member with creative skills to prepare the slides for the presentation in order to captivate the audience, especially in front of the bosses or the key personnel of an important client.

8. Time Management

Managers must handle multiple responsibilities, from project management, team management, communication, documentations etc. Therefore, time management skills are essential to prioritise tasks and meet deadlines. Good managers respect their own time, as well as others. They would never waste their time on unnecessary meetings that bring no value to the project delivery. They would say "No" to time wastage events, like the weekly business meeting which has the same agenda and attendees as the weekly departmental meeting. Yes, there are retards who would arrange meetings with the same agenda but with a different name just so they can waste their time at the office doing useless work.

For example, the manager sets priorities to the tasks, ensuring that urgent and critical matters are addressed promptly, while also allowing team members enough time to fulfil their responsibilities without feeling overwhelmed.

9.   Being Respectful

Good managers treat their team members with courtesy and listen to their ideas and concerns without dismissing or belittling them if those ideas are better than their own. They know it is a fundamental right for everyone to be respected regardless of their skin colour, preferences, gender or knowledge level. They would never steal those ideas, or the credits for the outstanding work done by the team. They would always give credit to the team members when due. Being respectful to others will earn trust from the team members, fostering a strong relationship and creating a high performing and loyal team that would always stand behind their manager during times of project crisis.

As an example, during team discussions, the manager actively listens to each team member's input and ensures that everyone's opinions are valued and taken into consideration before making the final decision.

10. Strong Adaptability Skills

A good manager is always adaptable to new changes and challenges. The business world is constantly evolving, resulting in new trends, processes and requirements. Things that were working well before might not have worked in current times. The manager will need to be observant and adapt to the changes if required so that they are always ready to manage possible risks that come along with those changes. Failure to take notice of the changes and adapt to them could cause issues to comply with the new regulations, and to remain competitive in the market against other competitors.

Example: When faced with changes in project requirements or unforeseen obstacles, the manager remains flexible and encourages the team to adjust their approach accordingly. If the tasks within the project requires changes to fit into the new regulation, the manager would plan ahead by performing the impact analysis and prepare the roadmap on how to complete the changes required.

11. Always Practise Transparency

Being open and transparent with the team fosters trust and encourages open communication. This is vital to ensure all parties are aligned on the objectives set by the management. When the manager practises transparency, issues could be raised timely to the respective parties to avoid jeopardising the entire project if the issue is serious enough. If the manager chooses to hide the issues and run the project in a non-transparent manner for fear of being penalised by the top management, then the manager risks causing the blame game afterwards where it will only create further delays to the project. Other team members and stakeholders will no longer place their trust further on someone who kept things behind them, making it much more difficult for the manager to get any support from them in the future.

Example: The manager shares company updates, changes in policies, and relevant information with the team promptly and honestly, keeping everyone informed about the organisation's direction. If there are any challenges or issues with the project, the manager would present them to the top management without hiding anything, along with the remedies to the problems so that the top management understands the situation and approves the proposals if needed.

12. Artful in Conflict Resolution

When there are more than one person working on a project, there tends to be conflict in ideas, preferences and ways of doing things. It is unavoidable especially if you have someone who tends to be aggressive when his or her ideas are not accepted by others.

As such, managers should be skilful in handling conflicts and disagreements among team members in a fair and constructive manner. Disagreements are pretty normal in a project setting as many would want to have their ideas implemented so they could claim credit for it, apart from the usual objections from the technical team due to the feasibility and difficulty of implementing a complex feature in a short timeframe. Regardless of the reasons, the manager ought to be careful in threading and managing these conflicts to avoid creating further confrontation and adding to the mess. The manager would need to find a balance and compromise for all parties since it would be impossible to satisfy all parties.

Example: In the event of a disagreement between team members, the manager acts as a mediator, facilitating the discussions, encouraging active listening, and guiding them towards finding a resolution that benefits all parties involved. All parties should be given the chance to voice out their ideas or feedback out of respect. The manager would then make the decision through the consensus, or having the final decision maker to decide on the final outcome.

13. Takes Accountability

A good manager takes responsibility for his or her actions and decisions, setting an example for the team to do the same. If mistakes were made, it is perfectly fine to admit to them and ensure that those mistakes are not repeated in the future. Having the courage to take on the responsibility and admitting to the mistakes will foster better relationships with others by gaining their trust. A manager who takes full accountability is looked upon favourably by other colleagues. Likewise, a manager who prefers to play the blame game will be despised by the rest.

Example: If a project doesn't meet its deadline, the manager acknowledges any oversight or miscommunication on their part and works with the team to understand what can be done differently in the next projects.

14. Development of Others

Effective managers are committed to the growth and development of their team members. They provide various opportunities for learning new skills or career advancement to the staff under their care. These managers fully understand that team members are the greatest asset. If the team members are given ample opportunities to grow and pick up new skills along the way, the team would be able to take on greater challenges and projects of bigger scale. This type of manager is willing to take the extra step and effort to polish every of his or her team members into shining diamonds.

Example: The manager identifies potentials within a junior team member and arranges for mentoring or coaching sessions to help the junior staff to sharpen his or her skills and gain more working experience by growing his or her role within the team. During the period, the manager observes the progress of each team member, noting down their strengths, weaknesses, work behaviour and preferences. When the company has new projects, the manager could take up those projects with the complexities that are suitable for the team, and delegate the tasks accordingly to the team members. With this, the team, along with the members will be able to advance further on their skills, gaining more experience and moving up the career ladder. Those teams that are comfortable remaining with the status quo, would see stagnant progress. That is when the staff of those teams began leaving one by one, or applying to switch to another department where they could see themselves advancing. There are also cases where some good staff leave the team or the company after finding no new challenges ahead in their career.

15. Positive Attitude

A positive attitude is contagious and can uplift the entire team, that is why laughter and good vibes spreads easily to an entire group of people. A good manager with a good amount of positive energy always feels optimistic towards the challenges faced by the team or project. The manager will take those challenges as means for the team to move to the next level. Likewise, negative energy should be avoided at all costs like the plague. If a manager is pessimistic and does not have the "can do" spirit within him or her, then the project could perhaps never see the light at the end because no one in the team will have the "oomph" to push the project through. The team members would also be influenced by the negative energy disseminating from the manager since the manager is the lead and pillar of the team. If the manager only complains about all the bad things that are happening to the project or to the team, e.g receiving complaints from other departments that the team is not pulling their weight in the project collaborations, they will see only daily impediments, obstacles, complaints and problems, rather than having that sense of triumph for completing and achieving a milestone in the project. When the good energy reaches zero, the team is as good as dead. It would be better to disband the team rather than having it stuck there wasting all the time and resources, unless the new manager or whoever taking over the team can once again pump in the much needed positive energy to give the team a new life and meaning.

Example: A good manager would instil positive energy into all of the team members, telling them to be resilient and the problems that arise would soon be resolved. The manager would also give his guarantee that things will be better, and if the obstacles are not cleared for the team to progress, he is sure that the upper management will assist in it after the escalation. He assures the team that the project will be completed and the team will be getting the credit and rewards for it.

16. Honesty

A good manager is always honest and transparent with their team or whomever he or she works with. Such a trait greatly fosters trust and credibility. At the workplace, apart from the skill sets needed for one to complete the work or tasks assigned, relationships are among the most important aspects in any company or organisation. Having good relationships with the clients and the public would bring in more business and revenues for the company, and likewise, having a good relationship among colleagues would create a better work environment and projects can run smoothly without much drama and conflicts. Honesty is the key ingredient in thr formula of everything you do in the company, be it between the manager and his or her team, or the top management and the low executives. When one is open and honest, others would be more eager to listen to him and help him out. Sometimes, your staff or co-workers would be more willing to share their feedback or ideas truthfully about the project, thereby allowing you to have more control on the project risks and its success.

Honesty is must for any manager as the team members are the pillars within a team. Being dishonest would break the pillars of trust and cause the entire team to crumble. I have witnessed the staff quit en masse within a team because the manager managed them through lies and deceit which created a lot of drama, conflict and blame game that was so bad until no one from the team was willing to show up at work.

Example: When the team faces setbacks, the manager communicates openly about the situation, acknowledges any mistakes made, and discusses plans to overcome challenges together. In return, the team may provide ideas and feedback on how to resolve the issues as soon as possible to get things back on track. Similarly, the manager will present the facts and issues to the upper management without hiding the bad stuff and showing only the good things. If there are issues that are causing delays to the project, the manager will present the problems, along with the solutions, if any, to the upper management to seek the approval to delay the project. Many a time, the manager would hide the problems and give pressure to the team to deliver the project on time, even if getting the team to work through the night.

17. Great Listening Skills

A good manager actively listens to their team members, taking their feedback and ideas into account. When problems arise within the project, the project manager will make the decision collectively and with consensus, if the solution or action taken will affect the entire team. If the manager decides to go with his or her own decision, the manager would at least present it to the team for feedback before any decision is made.

A manager's main job is to manage the team and the projects under the team. A manager's KPI is determined by how successful are the projects and the team being managed. Therefore it is a misconception that a manager should know everything, even though they have powers vested in them to give certain orders or commands. Most of the time, the manager would rely on the information from the team members who are more knowledgeable in certain domains or aspects, e.g coding, marketing etc. You can't expect the manager to change the requirement according to his own whim or instruct the developer to change the code or the system design based on the manager's desire, unless the manager has the required know-how and justification for doing so. Doing so will lead to the manager being seen as a tyrant or a micromanager, which is an undesirable trait that we discussed previously.

Most of the time, managers would first listen from all the team members, process the information, then proceed to make sound judgement or decision. By listening more to the team, it allows the team members to voice out the problems faced and possibly remedies to the problems. Being a good listener promotes respect among the team members where all feedback or ideas are taken in and consulted before any decision is made.

Example: During the weekly team meetings, the manager listens attentively to each team member's contributions, asking clarifying questions and seeking to understand different perspectives. The manager would then gather all the required information and make the decisions or proceed to escalate the problems to the upper management of the issues that cannot be resolved immediately within the manager's authority.

18. Ethical Behaviour

Good managers should demonstrate ethical behaviour and hold themselves to high moral standards. The manager would never get involved in bribing activities, either giving or receiving, or any other illegal actions that would bring benefits to the manager. It is quite easy for a manager to take advantage as they are often the middle man that liaises with external parties for a project. In some cases, project managers would also take charge of the vendor selection process, allowing them to take advantage by presenting the vendors who had given certain benefits to the manager as the only vendor choice for the project. Such unethical actions would result in serious implications to the company and the team, not just the manager alone. The entire team could be dragged into a criminal investigation because of the actions of that one unethical manager.

Example: The manager upholds ethical practices in the team's work and ensures that all decisions align with the organisation's values and principles. The manager knew if he or she is implicated in the illegal actions, it could very well affect the entire team, including causing the team to lose their livelihood if the entire team is disbanded after the dismissal of the manager in order for the company to set an example to the rest of the staff members.

19. Creative Mindset

Having a creative mindset is one of the desirable traits of a manager. This type of manager is always open to new ideas and approaches that can help the manager to find innovative solutions to problems. Managers who are creative usually would be more keen to "think outside the box" than following the existing, sometimes archaic ways of doing things within the company that were left by the seniors. They would try out new methods and learn from the mistakes, or what went well and then adapt to the situation to formulate the best action plan. Having a creative manager could also help to create a better environment for the team as the manager will encourage the team members to share their ideas for a project or a problem. A creative work environment would spur great ideas and never leave a dull moment, giving the team members a more enjoyable experience at work as it provides the much needed brain stimulation and motivation to come to work everyday.

Example: When faced with a complex challenge, the manager encourages the team to think outside the box, inviting diverse ideas and exploring unconventional solutions. A problem can be resolved in different ways, just like how a chicken can be cooked in different methods. It can be deep fried, stir-fried, baked, steamed, etc. The team member with the best idea voted by the rest will be given a small reward and credit will be given if the contribution is acknowledged by the upper management. The manager could get the team members into role playing to find the best solution or design for a product.

20. Calm Under Pressure

In challenging situations, a manager remains composed and makes rational decisions despite the overwhelming odds. A manager who crumbles under pressure, or panics easily would only display weak leadership which is not befitting the role of a person that is tasked to lead and manage the team. Such weakness would allow others to exploit the manager or the team for their own gains. A good manager would always be calm to show that he or she is always in control regardless of how bad the situation is.

Example: During a crisis or high-pressure project deadlines, the manager stays calm, assesses the situation methodically, and guides the team toward a resolution without panicking. Despite the continued pressure from the top management to rush the project, the manager provided them with the consequences post project implementation if the issues raised were not addressed adequately. The manager would also ask the top management to acknowledge the risks involved should they demand the project to be rushed and rolled out with the unsolved issues. On the contrary, the bad manager who succumbs to the pressure would just get the team members to work day and night in order to rush the project off where the team would get the blame later for the bad quality delivered, where they will then have to work through sleepless nights to clean up the mess again, all because the manager could not hold the pressure and the need to please the top management.

What is a project management methodology and why is it important?

A project management methodology is a structured approach or framework for planning, executing, monitoring, and controlling projects. It provides a set of best practices, guidelines, processes, and tools to help project managers and teams efficiently and effectively manage projects from initiation to completion. Project management methodologies are critical for ensuring that projects are delivered on time, within budget, and with the expected quality and scope.

Key benefits of having a project management methodology when managing a project:

- **Consistency**: A methodology establishes a standardised approach to managing projects. This consistency ensures that all team members are on the same page and follow a common set of processes and practices.

- **Efficiency:** Project management methodologies offer templates, tools, and predefined processes that can help streamline project execution. This can save time and reduce the risk of errors.

- **Quality**: By following established best practices, methodologies help improve the quality of project deliverables and outcomes. They provide a structured way to identify and manage risks, issues, and changes, leading to better project results.

- **Communication**: A methodology often includes communication and reporting guidelines, ensuring that project stakeholders are informed of project status, progress, and issues. This promotes transparency and effective communication.

- **Risk Management**: Methodologies include risk management processes that help identify, assess, and mitigate risks early in the project lifecycle, reducing the likelihood of costly issues arising later on.

- **Scope Management**: Methodologies assist in defining and controlling project scope, preventing scope creep and ensuring that the project stays on track.

- **Resource Allocation**: Some project methodologies offer guidance on resource allocation, helping organisations allocate resources effectively and avoid overloading team members..

- **Stakeholder Engagement**: Methodologies typically include strategies for engaging and managing project stakeholders, which is crucial for the project success.

- **Learning and Improvement**: Project management methodologies encourage a culture of continuous improvement. After each project, lessons learned are documented and can be applied to future projects, enhancing overall project management capabilities.

- **Scalability**: Many methodologies are scalable, which means they can be adapted to different project sizes and complexities. This flexibility allows companies or organisations to use the same framework for various types of projects.

- **Compliance and Standards:** Certain industries or organisations may have regulatory or quality standards that require adherence. Project management methodologies can help ensure that projects align with these standards.

Choose your own Project Management Methodologies

There are various project management methodologies out there to help you to facilitate the tasks and ensure that the projects run smoothly. Some managers swear by only one methodology and will apply it on every project, regardless of the situations. Though they do mostly work well since many have applied it on their projects, there is a catch on using them, similar to taking paracetamol when you have cold or flu symptoms. It might help to alleviate some discomfort, but taking the right medicine would help cure the symptoms quicker. Take for example, if you have a complicated project involving multiple stakeholders that keep changing their mind, and your top management wishes to see updates every week, which methodology would you be adopting for your project?

Waterfall Methodology

The Waterfall methodology is a traditional, sequential approach to project management. It follows a linear progression of phases, where each phase is completed before moving on to the next one. The phases typically include requirements gathering, design, implementation, testing, deployment, and maintenance. Waterfall is characterised by its structured and planned nature, with limited flexibility for changes once a phase is completed.

Pros:

- Clear structure and defined phases provide a systematic approach to project management.

- Well-suited for projects with stable requirements and little expected changes.

- Progress is easily measurable at each phase.

- Documentation is comprehensive and detailed.

Cons:

- Limited flexibility for changes or adjustments once a phase is completed.

- High risk of late-stage rework if initial requirements were misunderstood or not well-defined, or changes from stakeholders that require revamp to the original requirements.

- Limited customer involvement until the final stage, which may lead to misalignment of expectations.

- Difficult to accommodate new requirements or emerging trends during the project.

Agile Methodology

Agile is an iterative and flexible approach to managing a project. It focuses on collaboration, adaptability, and delivering incremental value. Agile methodologies, such as Scrum and KANBAN, break projects into smaller time-bound iterations known as Sprints. The team works on prioritised tasks, continuously reviews progress, and adjusts plans based on feedback. Agile promotes customer involvement, regular communication, and embraces change to improve the final product.

Pros:

- Emphasises flexibility and adaptability to change of expectations and requirements.

- Regular feedback loops and customer involvement improve the final product's quality.

- Allows for continuous improvement and the ability to refine project priorities.

- Encourages collaboration and self-organising teams.

Cons:

- Requires active involvement and availability of stakeholders throughout the project, from requirements gathering, grooming, development and testing.

- May not be suitable for projects with fixed deadlines or rigid requirements.

- Lack of comprehensive documentation can be challenging for long-term maintenance or handover, since all of the tasks or work are documented as Epics and stories.

- Requires experienced team members who are familiar with Agile principles and practices to unlock the full potential and team productivity. Otherwise, most will see the tasks such as sprint planning, story point assignments, daily stand-ups and retrospective sessions as nothing more than additional workload to them.

Lean Methodology

The key objective of the Lean methodology is to minimise waste and maximise value for stakeholders. It first originated in the manufacturing sector but has since been adapted for project management. The Lean methodology focuses on streamlining processes, reducing unnecessary activities, and improving efficiency. It emphasises continuous improvement and involves stakeholders in identifying and eliminating non-value-adding tasks or resources. In other words, managers would focus on key tasks and discard any activities that are deemed of no added value to the overall project.

Pros:

- Focuses on eliminating waste, improving efficiency, and reducing costs.

- Streamlines processes, leading to increased productivity.

- Enhances customer value and satisfaction through continuous improvement.

- Increases team collaboration and involvement in process improvement.

Cons:

- Requires a thorough understanding of processes and value stream mapping.

- May face resistance to change and scepticism from team members.

- The emphasis on efficiency may prioritise short-term gains over long-term strategic goals.

- May be challenging to apply in projects with a high degree of uncertainty or creativity.

Critical Path Method (CPM)

The Critical Path Method is a technique used to schedule and manage complex projects. It identifies the critical path, which is the sequence of activities that determines the project's overall duration. The Critical Path Method (CPM) uses a network diagram to visualise the project's activities, their dependencies, and the expected duration for each task. It helps the project managers to identify activities that have slack time and prioritise tasks to ensure the project always stays on schedule.

Pros:

- Identifies the critical path, allowing the project managers to prioritise important/critical tasks and allocate resources effectively.

- Provides a clear timeline and helps identify potential bottlenecks or risks.

- Enables effective scheduling and project coordination.

- Facilitates monitoring and control of project progress.

Cons:

- Requires accurate task duration estimation for reliable scheduling. Wrong estimates would create a snowball effect and contribute to the delay of the project.

- May not accommodate changes or unexpected events well since the project duration and timely completion is key.

- Focuses primarily on time management and may overlook other project aspects.

- Complexity increases with larger projects or those with numerous dependencies.

- Not suitable for projects with unconfirmed/unrefined requirements that could change every time.

PRINCE2 (Projects IN Controlled Environments)

PRINCE2 is a process-based project management methodology that is widely used in the United Kingdom and other western countries. Though other countries are beginning to adopt it over the years. The methodology provides a structured approach for managing projects, emphasising the importance of clear roles, responsibilities, and project governance. PRINCE2 divides projects into stages and incorporates several principles, such as continued business justification, defined roles and responsibilities, and a focus on managing exceptions and risks.

Pros:

- Provides a structured framework for project management, ensuring consistent practices.

- Emphasises clear roles, responsibilities, and communication channels.

- Enables effective project governance and control.

- Supports efficient project planning and risk management.

Cons:

- Can be bureaucratic and time-consuming at times, particularly for small projects.

- May not be suitable for highly dynamic or innovative projects.

- Requires a detailed understanding of the methodology and its processes.

- May lack the flexibility needed to respond quickly to unexpected changes.

Six Sigma

Six Sigma was originally developed for quality management. Now, the method is being applied to project management as well. Six Sigma aims to minimise defects or errors and improve overall process performance. The method utilises statistical analysis and data-driven techniques to measure, analyse, improve, and control project processes. It follows a defined set of phases, known as DMAIC (Define, Measure, Analyse, Improve, Control), to achieve process improvement and project success.

Pros:

- Focuses on data-driven decision making and process improvement.

- Enhances quality control and reduces defects.

- Provides a structured methodology to identify and eliminate inefficiencies.

- Improves customer satisfaction and increases overall process efficiency.

Cons:

- Requires a significant investment in training and expertise.

- Can be time-consuming, particularly during the data collection and analysis phases.

- May not be suitable for projects with a high level of uncertainty or creativity.

- Focuses primarily on process improvement and may overlook other project management aspects.

If you are interested in the details of any of the project management methodologies above, you may look through them online. Otherwise you may register for those online courses to have a mentor to guide you through the implementation. Some of them provide professional certifications where you might have to sit for exams in order to be certified. If you ask me, certification is not the priority, but the actual experience in utilising and implementing projects using the methodology with great results matters more.

Personally, I am an avid supporter of the Agile SCRUM methodology. It gave me the perfect balance and flexibility in managing projects and empowering my team through the daily standup and retrospective sessions. Having said that, it doesn't mean that I have to apply this methodology every single time. There are times where the Waterfall methodology works just as well, particularly small projects with confirmed requirements. The key to good project management is to always be flexible and open to various strategies to achieve the goals and deliver that project successfully.

It is fine to mix and match various methods to form the methodology that works best for you. There is no right or wrong with them as they are merely guidelines for references since they have been applied to different projects with varying complexities and setup. Cultural differences can be a factor as well in determining the effectiveness of the methodology that you apply for your team. This is true in Asian countries where the junior staff is taught to follow all the orders given by their superiors and usually have very little opportunity to voice out their opinions regarding the project. In this case, a waterfall methodology could be the better option, with a retrospective session thrown in every week, or after the completion of the project.

Case Study 1

There was a project team transformation case that went very well during one of my stints as a lead product manager. When I joined that company, I was tasked with planning, designing and developing new solutions that would be replacing the current products that were running on old technologies. Those solutions required a sizeable resource to maintain, with ever growing technical debts and vulnerabilities. It became too costly for the company to continue using them and the management decided that it was finally time to replace those systems in order plug the wastage and reduce the operation costs.

My manager, who happened to be the head of the department at that time, did not allocate any resources for my new projects even though the top management had made the decision. I had to tap into the existing resource pool of developers whose daily job was to fix bugs that were reported by the customer service team. It was a complete mess. To make matters worse, the project managers were using only the waterfall methodology as the only project management process for everything. To make matters worse, the top management wanted to see weekly progress updates on the new products. In summary, there was no dedicated team to focus on the new product development. I was told to get developers who have the additional time for my projects. I have a feeling that the head of department wanted the new initiative to fall badly because he tried to revamp the systems a couple of times before without success. Now, he is definitely not going to let some newcomer complete the project with flying colours for fear of losing his position in the company. That, however, was purely my assumption. I did not care much about all the office politics that were going in at that time. My only goal was to complete the project assigned to me, the very reason that the company hired me in the first place.

After assessing the team structure and the process, I found them to be extremely inefficient. A team of more than fifty developers could only clear off about twenty tickets a week. Furthermore, most of the tickets were small tasks like UI changes or adding small features to the existing systems.

Here's a summary of the problems:

1. Only one tech lead to delegate the work or tasks to the developers. If the tech lead is not around, then no work will be assigned for the day. The tech lead would spend most of his team arranging the work for the developers, which means there is no time for him to do

his actual work, e.g performing code reviews, or working on more complex problems.

2. There was no prioritisation of the tasks by the project managers. They would just throw in the change requests, issues, new feature requests etc to the tech lead every week to arrange for the development and roll out. It was more of a first-in-first-out queue system. This often led to massive complaints from the business units as certain changes or features were required to satisfy the new compliance and regulations set by the government. Failure to adhere to those rules would result in hefty fines by the government.

3. Tasks were not measured against the staff experience. Sometimes complex tasks or issues were assigned to junior developers who had a difficult time in completing the tasks on time. The delays brought condemnation from the project managers and stakeholders, resulting in high turnover rate for junior staff members who could be trained into super star workers.

4. There were many cases of severe underestimation of the tasks by the project managers. Most of the project managers do not have any technical background.

Those who did have some technical knowledge were incompetent developers that previously failed at their jobs, so they would give a far higher effort estimate for some simple tasks, giving the illusion that those tasks were massive undertakings. These managers often set a timeframe for the tasks by "plucking the figure from the sky" without first consulting with the developers who had the in-depth knowledge on the inner workings of the system, and who would be the ones doing the job.

5. No will from the head of department to transform the old culture and the rotten process. Many of the managers preferred to maintain the status quo as they could hide their incompetence since the current process somehow "empowered" them to do anything they want without any check and balance.

6. Some good developers who are able to complete their tasks were given more work, because well, they could complete it on time. This has caused a severe imbalance in the staff workload. The good staff were overworked, while the not so great staff could be rewarded with no work while still getting paid. There was no KPI set for each staff member.

Something had to be done to change the broken system. After weeks of negotiations and persuasion, along with the threat of my resignation thrown into the mix, the head of department finally agreed to give me a free hand in revamping the whole team structure and its processes. Initially there was stiff resistance from some of the project managers, especially one who "acted" as the lead for the project managers, when in fact she wasn't. Since I had the blessing from the head of department, I gave a notice to all those who resisted the change; either go through the transformation or go through the exit door.

The first thing to change was the process itself. The waterfall methodology and the current way of having the tech lead managing the task delegation bit must go. It had to be replaced with a more flexible and efficient process suited for the current setting. I opted to go with the Agile SCRUM way. We set up JIRA, one of my favourite project management tools available in the market, and configured it to run the SCRUM methodology with all the functions to create epics, stories and what not, along with a large dashboard showing the tasks and the sprints. After all preparations were completed, we began testing out the new process with a dozen developers by forming the first ever SCRUM team in the company. The rest of the developers would still be using the old way. This is done so that we can present to the head of department on the differences between the old and the new process, and that the change would significantly increase the productivity of the team.

For my style, I would prefer to begin the week with the Sprint Planning with the developers. The stories in the backlog would have been groomed with the stakeholders in the previous week. I opted for a weekly sprint as a start, so I may get the team feedback along with the things that worked out for the team, and things that didn't or require improvement during our retrospective session on Friday, before the week ends. The reason for starting the Sprint Planning on a Monday was to get the developers to start on a fresh mind, and knowing what to complete by the end of the week. After the retrospective session on Friday, they can go and enjoy their weekend without thinking about the work and start again on Monday. The sprint planning session was always timeboxed to 1 hour. If there are stories that require further clarifications, they would be discussed in separate sessions with the respective stakeholders. The developers would discuss stories and assign a story point to each of the stories, with consensus via voting. For example, a junior developer might think the task or story is worth 5 story points, as he or she is not familiar with it while a senior developer might think the task or story is worth only 1 story point. When there is a stark contrast in the story points voted (you can use a free tool online to facilitate the story point voting, like Planning Poker, PlanITPoker, etc.), the ones giving the highest and the lowest points will have to provide justifications on the story points given. This is to allow the seniors to show to the junior developers that there is an easier way to complete the task. The same goes the other way round where the developers who had been working on that module could justify the complications and the actual effort needed to the rest of the developers in a more accurate manner. With this, we could reduce or eliminate the problems where a task is grossly overestimated or underestimated by the project managers. After the team has completed the Sprint Planning session, they would start picking up the stories to work on for the week. From there onwards we would have daily stand ups that were time-boxed to 15 minutes for the team to inform the rest on their tasks for the day, progress update and also any challenges or obstacles that could be showstoppers or delaying their progress.

The daily stand-ups were effective for a manager to track the progress from the team consistently without being an annoyance to the team who is already busy. A lot of the managers would ask the team members to provide them with their staff members' progress updates as and when they need it because they are either being asked by their superiors or they are having the weekly management meeting. I have seen many bad managers who would get the entire team to stop their work just to prepare and compile their progress update report. With the daily stand-ups, the managers could easily track the progress and compile them. After all, this is the job of a manager. With the daily stand-ups, it is useful in identifying the impediments from the team and immediately taking action to resolve them. The team could be having some issues with the requirement given, or they have some blockers that are preventing them from completing their job. If the issues cannot be rectified immediately, then the manager could re-prioritise the task and get the team to work on other issues, instead of having the team to do nothing while waiting for the issue to be resolved. Another great thing about the process is that everyone could see what the other member is working on.

After having the Agile SCRUM process implemented for a week, the result was incredible. Productivity had increased by more than 60%, and the first SCRUM team managed to complete as many tickets as the rest of the team. Mind you, we had only 12 members in the SCRUM team, among the fifty plus staff in the department. The second week onwards, the SCRUM team was completing more than double of the tickets. Task assignment was automated with the SCRUM process. The staff members no longer need to wait for the tech lead to assign the tasks to them. If a staff finished his or her tasks ahead, then the staff could pick up the next ticket from the sprint board, or even request the project manager to add in tasks from the upcoming sprints if there are no more tickets left on the board to be worked on. This has allowed better progress as everyone would have tasks to be worked on. It would be a "gang-bang" if any of the staff reported "no tasks to be completed for the day" during the daily standup. It became an unspoken rule that everyone needs to be busy everyday, which to me is an "excellent" rule. Also if any of the staff completes more tasks than assigned for the sprint, then the staff could take on easier tasks in the next sprint. There was a "debt" collection process among the developers to give or take up more tasks, in order to repay the "debt" from the previous week. It was an interesting experience as there were funny times where the team members would "negotiate" on how to repay the "debts" during the sprint planning sessions. This kind of humourous and harmonious teamwork greatly improved the working relationship among the staff where before this, staff would be complaining about the workload disparity among them.

With the huge improvements to the overall productivity and efficiency of the department, the head of the department granted me the absolute authority to restructure the resources of the entire department, modelled after the success of the first SCRUM team. To have fifty plus members in one team might reduce the effectiveness and efficiency of the team as the Sprint Planning and Daily standup sessions that were time-boxed to an hour and 15 minutes respectively will not be sufficient for the team size. Therefore, the next action taken was to break down the team into smaller SCRUM teams, each complete with a tech lead and a product manager, who would double as the project manager for the SCRUM team as well.

The entire department was broken into the following teams:

- SCRUM team One - original Scrum team

- SCRUM team Two

- SCRUM team Three

- SCRUM team Four

We started off with the same process for all the teams in order to get the rest of the team members to adopt and familiarise themselves with the new process. On top of the team structure, I formed a committee of the product managers where we would review the requirements, groom the stories and assign them to the respective teams to work on as part of their sprints. From there we could identify the strength of each team, which we could plan and utilise them for specific roles in the future. Apart from that, the committee would be meeting and discussing the work allocation to ensure that the workload could be spread more evenly between the teams, and not having the top performing team to take up most of the tasks. Of course the tasks allocated will be according to the capabilities of the team members within each of the SCRUM team. For example, team one has more seasoned and experienced developers. Hence, team one will take on more difficult tasks such as new feature development, module revamp and core function debugging. The junior programmers will take on UI related issues or simpler tasks. Since the team KPI is measured by the completion of story points, there was no conflict where one would argue that he or she completed more tasks or tickets than the rest as compared to the previous process. Everyone understands his or her role and responsibilities. After giving the task assignment job back to the project management team, the tech lead is now able to focus on code review related tasks, guiding and training the rest of the developers to ensure that the system adheres to good coding practice and the solution design fulfils all the standards and compliance required.

With just a month into the new process, the department was able to complete six times more tickets than the previous setup. Furthermore, the teams started to clean up and complete the tasks that were created years ago. We even managed to finish off three big features that were scheduled two years ago. Once every team member completely adopted the new process, it was time to start defining the specific roles for each of the SCRUM team. Since the first team consisted mostly of the senior developers, I started assigning small projects and new feature development to them. Team Two would take up more change requests and bug fixing tasks while Team Three and Team Four would take up on smaller change requests, UI/UX related issues and support related tickets that includes data maintenance and system design investigations. After the second month, I formed a new team, Team ZERO, composed of developers, QA testers and product managers who have shown great curiosity and passion about developing a new platform with up-to-date technologies in order to resolve all the legacy issues that were plaguing the production system. The main roles and responsibilities of Team ZERO were to:

1. Propose new solutions and features

2. Research on new technologies

3. Develop prototypes

4. Roll out new systems

Apart from the official roles above, Team ZERO will also act as the technical consultants to other teams on best programming practices, perform code reviews and provide guidance to the junior teams. The secondary role was to produce a second "Team ZERO" that can help to guide other teams and take on heavier responsibilities. The committee of product managers were also given the extended role of providing solutions to problems or requirements gathered from business users and stakeholders through the weekly brainstorming sessions. The proposals that were passed by consensus were then added into the main product backlog for further grooming, after which they would be assigned to the respective Scrum teams accordingly.

The team revamp was a great success. Productivity improved significantly. The new structure and process allowed the teams to complete close to 10 times the amount of tickets when compared to the original team running on the Waterfall methodology. The teams were able to work on large tickers that were shelved for years in the backlog as well, a feat that no one think possible before that. The teams managed to roll out new features that were longed for by the customer service and operation teams to reduce unnecessary workload and increase the efficiency of the process that led to improved overall customer satisfaction. Due to the success, other committees were formed: technical committee, data security committee etc. Each committee would meet up regularly to review the issues or challenges faced by the organisation and draw up a plan or roadmap to address them.

The positive effect from the structural change to the It department even prompted some other departments to adopt a similar approach when restructuring their teams, which I considered to be one of my great achievements in instilling a more positive working culture in the organisation. The most important thing of all, the previous toxic working environment was eradicated, replacing it with a more staff-friendly environment that emphasises on transparency, harmony, trust and honesty.

Case Study 2

The second case study involves a team without any experience in system design but was formed by the management to lead the digital transformation initiatives for the organisation. The company had put together a brand new team hastily to look into digitising the company process to keep up with the digital era and for the company to keep up with the competitors. Each team member comes from a different background. We have one from finance, one from audit, one from customer service and one from digital marketing. However, we have none from IT, or even someone with an ounce of technical knowledge to put things together to form the "to be " solution or create new system proposals for the management to consider. Everyone was doing his or her own things without much interaction. Each member worked within his or her own silo and roadmap. They were creating proposals from their own perspectives. The previous head of department failed to put them to good use, often complaining about how ineffective, or useless they were when in fact the head of department was supposed to lead them. Eventually, the head of department resigned as he couldn't show any progress and positive results to the management. The company eventually contacted me, through a friend working in the company, to come in and assist them with the new department since I had the technical skills required, and the portfolio that fits perfectly into the puzzle for the department.

Once I came on board the new team, the first thing I did was to conduct an interview session with each of the team members before rushing in to prepare the project timelines, roadmaps and what not. This first step is vital as it would allow me to:

- to know the team members better, especially their strengths and weaknesses

- to start forming a work relationship with them

- to set the expectations with them moving forward

- to learn from their past working experiences with the company

After knowing them a bit better and gaining valuable insights about the company, the next step was to formulate a strategy on how to structure the team and utilise the key strengths of each team member. The organisation had the vision and intention to transform all their manual processes into a digital one in order to maximise productivity, increase the process efficiency, better resource allocation, reduce human errors and operation costs. It was a huge undertaking. There were many different processes that needed to be re-worked on, from procurement, supply chain management, document management etc. We set off by digitising the procurement and invoicing process as our first targets for digitisation initiative since it will create the biggest value for the company in terms of cost reduction; by reducing the need for physical documents, courier service and paper storage fees. It would also greatly improve the payment process efficiency for both the company and the suppliers. It was a win-win situation. I started the project by getting the team member who hailed from the finance department to prepare the "to-be" process flow and then having the team member from the audit team to review the process in order to ensure that the process flow and requirements adhere to the company policies, rules, regulations, compliance and law of the country. With that completed, I would have completed the operation flow to be used as a reference for the system design.

Next, I had the team member with the customer service experience to map out all the complaints and the common issues reported by the suppliers pertaining to the current procurement and invoicing process. As for the team member with the digital marketing background, I had him role play as a supplier to review if the new process and the "would-be" system could meet our goals for cost reduction and improved the operation efficiency while providing better experience for the suppliers when dealing with the company. The team member from digital marketing, after experiencing the process, could then think of effective ways to promote the new process to internal staff as well as our external suppliers.

At this point, all the team members were able to contribute positively to the project as they already had the experience in managing the tasks given to them. Instead of running like a headless chicken with no clear direction, they were able to focus on the assignments where they could leverage on their knowledge and past experience, giving them a less stressful work environment. After we had gathered all the necessary information, we began preparing the proposal for the new system that incorporated the desired features and the new process flow that would replace the existing one.

The next challenge was to seek the approval and buy-in from the top management to overhaul the existing process. It wasn't easy as the top management threw a lot of questions and scenarios to test out the new process. After weeks of a game of tug-of-war with the management, revising the presentation slides for more than twenty times after getting feedback from the management, we finally managed to get the green light to go ahead with the implementation of the proposal.

We put together a document of close to nine hundred pages, with every business rules and scenarios required for the system and then pass it to the IT department to source for a vendor in order to implement the new solution. Along the way, we participated in the vendor sourcing process, requirement gathering workshops and quality testing. Everyone in the team was in high spirits to get the first ever digitisation project completed as perfectly as possible. However, in reality, nothing is perfect. There were some hiccups and obstacles along the way, which were common in projects of any scale. The bigger scale of a project, the more issues one would have to resolve as the problems are not limited to just the requirements, it could be people that we work with. Some people are born just to annoy the heck out of you by rejecting everything except their own ideas. We had a few of those in the company. They would give a million reasons on why the process would not have worked when in fact, we had simulated most of the scenarios. Their reason given was, "because they know." As a word of advice, it is perfectly fine to ignore this type of idiot who contributes nothing but trouble.

After 6 months of hard work with lots of communications between the departments and the software vendor, we managed to get the new system up after another month of rigorous testing. It was the first big project that the company had since many years ago which was within the acceptable budget and timeline. Of course it did incur some additional expenses as there were new requirements added to the original scope that were deemed a priority to be included in the launch. The development timeline was extended twice to factor in these new changes. There were some delays in the development schedule due to some miscommunications between the business users and software vendors, along with a few technical problems that required a bit more time to resolve. All in all, the project was considered a success.

Key factors that contributed to the successful roll out were:

1.   We had ensured that there were transparency in communication between departments and the upper management. All issues were reported to the top management without any modifications by any parties to make it look good to the top management. This allowed the top management to make accurate decisions in resolving the problems faced by the team.

2.   We had very good support from the top management who listened to the feedback and made the decisions decisively. This greatly reduces conflicts, especially when it comes to different ideas to the new system.

Apart from that, the top management helped to shut down the critics who refused changes to the old, inefficient process.

3.   We respected the views and ideas from all who were involved in the project. Everyone was able to voice out their opinions on the proposal, what could be better and what features they think would help them in their work. As for the few bad apples who tried to sabotage the project due to jealousy, their feedback was still recorded but was put in a backlog that might never see the light. This was done just to appease them to avoid deeper conflicts that could cause unwanted delay to the project.

4.   No one in the team was trying to claim all the credit or discredit the work of others. Everyone was respectful and worked towards a common goal with a positive attitude despite facing many challenges over the course of the project.

In the next few months, we kept the momentum going and completed a couple more projects. The team had received not only gratitude from staff from other departments for greatly reducing their workload with the new system, but compliments from our suppliers as well because the new invoicing system enabled immediate payment processing if there were no disputes found in the invoice submitted against the purchase order raised by the company. Rather than having to wait for the finance team to perform the manual checking that could take up to 30 business days before the payment can be released to the suppliers, now with the new system, the suppliers can be paid within 5 business days.

The team's hard work had finally paid off at the end of the year. During the company's annual dinner, our team was awarded with the "Excellent Team of the Year " and "The Most Innovative" awards. Each team member was given additional monetary rewards on top of the annual increment and bonuses for the good job done for the company.

Final Words

A manager for a team or a department is akin to a Captain of a ship. If you are the Head of a department, then you are commanding a fleet of ships.

Take for example, if you are the captain of the ship, you would be relying a lot on your crews to manage different jobs on the ship. As the captain, you would steer the ship towards your goals, e.g. finding land to resupply, navigating through the hostile sea or even engaging enemy ships. I always paint this image for my staff members. Imagine when there is a battle going on with an enemy vessel, as the captain of the ship, you would take in information from the lookout to determine the direction of the enemy ship, then steer the ship so that your gunners could fire at the ships with all the cannons, in order to maximise firepower on the enemy. If the captain is having all the bad traits mentioned above, like being a micromanager, and doesn't listen to the crew members, how would the battle turn out? The captain would be busy telling the gunners how much gunpowder they need and which cannon balls to use, instead of steering the ship well. The outcome of the battle would be obvious.

Reality is no different. When you are the captain of your team, you will always need to take command and display strong leadership, while showing respect to your fellow crew mates to ensure the team's success. Your responsibilities lie not in managing the work of your team members, but managing the team members so they can shine brightest and be the best at their work.

Hope the tips above assist you in some ways if you are applying for a management role.

Good luck!

About the Author

Kyle C. is an entrepreneur, investor, and middle-class worker who has worked with various companies across different regions around the world. Equipped with his knowledge, he began his life as an amateur writer to produce some writings based on his personal experiences so that he could share his stories with a wider audience as compared to a selected few among his circle of friends.

Other books by this Author:

1. *Layman's Guide to Investing, with a bit of common sense (2020)*

2. *How to Get Rich, by understanding the economy (2020)*

3. *Words for Humanity (2020)*

4. *My Weight Loss Journey, Without Spending a Single Dime (2021)*

5. *How to Create A Good Product (2021)*

6. *You Should Start Thinking About Yourself, For Once (2021)*

7. *Why I Have No Savings & How to Start Saving Up (2021)*

8. *How to become a Great Business Analyst (2022)*

9. *14 Ghost Short Stories (2022)*

10. *Our Deepest Desire In Life - Freedom (2022)*

11. *How to become a Sales Grand Master (2022)*